American Lives

Jesse Jackson

Jennifer Blizin Gillis

Heinemann Library
Chicago, Illinois

Designed by Q2A Creative

Printed in China by WKT Limited

10 09 08 07 06
10 9 8 7 6 5 4 3 2 1

Library of Congress Cataloging-in-Publication Data
Gillis, Jennifer Blizin, 1950-
   Jesse Jackson/Jennifer Blizin Gillis.
      p. cm. – (American lives)
   Includes bibliographical references and index.
   ISBN 1-4034-6983-0 (hc) – ISBN 1-4034-6990-3
      (pb)
   1. Jackson, Jesse, 1941 – Juvenile literature.
2. African Americans – Biography – Juvenile
literature. 3. Civil rights workers – United States –
Biography – Juvenile literature. 4. Presidential
candidates – United States – Biography – Juvenile
literature. I. Title. II. Series: American lives
(Heinemann Library (Firm))

   E185.97.J25G55 2006
   973.927'092 – dc22

                              2005010327

JB
JACKSON, J.
   C. 1

Acknowledgments
The author and publishers are grateful to the
following for permission to reproduce copyright
material:

AP/Wide World Photos pp. **16**, **19**, **26**; Corbis pp. **5**
(Jacques M. Chenet), **20** (Wally McNamee), **29** (Rune
Hellestad); Corbis/Bettmann pp. **17**, **21**; Getty
Images/AFP pp. **25**, **28** (Tim Sloan); Getty
Images/Hulton Archive p. **12**; Getty Images/Time
Life Pictures pp. **24**, **7** (Ralph Morse), **11** (Michael
Mauney), **18** (Arnold H. Drapkin), **22** (Diana
Walker), **23**(Steve Liss), **27** (Cynthia Johnson);
Granger Collection p. **15**; Greenville Cultural
Exchange pp. **6**, **8**, **9**, **10**; Magnum Photos pp. **4**
(Elliot Erwitt),**13**, **14** (Bob Adelman).

Cover photograph of Jesse Jackson reproduced with
permission of Corbis/William Coupon.

Every effort has been made to contact copyright
holders of any material reproduced in this book.
Any omissions will be rectified in subsequent
printings if notice is given to the publisher.

Some words are shown in bold, **like this**. You can
find out what they mean by looking in the glossary.

Contents

A Bad Scare

In the 1940s, some young black children went into a neighborhood store. They wanted to buy some candy. It was a busy day, and the store was crowded with people. The children grew tired of waiting their turn.

One of the boys was named Jesse. He thought the store's owner was his friend. So, Jesse whistled to get his attention. Suddenly, the noisy store got very quiet.

Until the 1960s, unfair laws kept African Americans apart from white people.

Jesse Jackson continues to fight for civil rights for all Americans and for people around the world.

The storeowner reached under the counter and pulled out a gun. He pointed it at Jesse and said, "Never whistle at a white man." Jesse ran out of the store.

Jesse never forgot that moment. He grew up to work for **civil rights** for African Americans. He grew up to be the first African American to ever run for President of the United States.

Childhood

Jesse Jackson was born October 8, 1941 in Greenville, South Carolina. His mother, Helen Burns, was not married when she had Jesse. In those days, that could ruin a woman's life. She was asked to leave her church.

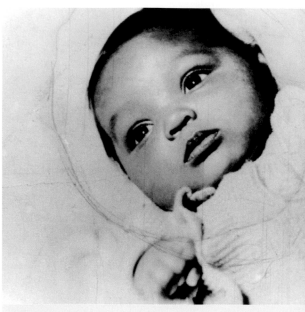

This picture of Jesse as a baby was taken in 1941.

Jesse was two when his mother married Charles Jackson. When he was very young, Jesse thought Charles was his real father. But most people in town knew that his real father was Helen's neighbor, Noah Robinson.

The Life of Jesse Jackson

1941	1957	1963	1964	1965	1971
Jesse Jackson born October 8	Adopted by stepfather, Charles	Marries Jacqueline	Graduates from NC A&T	Goes to work for **SCLC**	Leaves the SCLC to start his own **civil rights** group

Other children said mean things to Jesse. They called him a nobody because he did not know who his real father was. Jesse's grandmother told him that someday he would be somebody.

Jesse's family was very religious. He liked hearing stories from the Bible. Jesse was already a good speaker. He won a prize for preaching a **sermon** in Sunday School. He wanted to become a **minister**.

This is a picture of Greenville, South Carolina in the 1940s.

A School Star

There were very few good jobs for African Americans in the South. Jesse's grandmother could not read or write, but she knew a good education was important. She told Jesse to work hard in school so he could get a good job. Jesse joined a reading club at a separate library for black people. In ninth grade he was president of his class.

Jesse always had part-time jobs, too. At first Jesse worked in a lumberyard. Later, he worked as a waiter and worked at a bakery.

Jesse was a very good student. He worked hard outside of class, too.

Jesse was the **quarterback** for his high school football team. When he graduated, the New York Giants football team offered him a job. Jesse knew the team had offered a white student a job, too. He found

Jesse played football, basketball, and baseball in high school. He is number 25 in this picture of the basketball team.

out that the white student was going to earn ten times the money they promised him! Jesse decided to go to college and play football for a Big Ten University.

He got a **scholarship** to the University of Illinois at Chicago. In the South, African Americans were not allowed to go to school with white people. The University of Illinois had black and white students. Jesse thought he would have more freedom there.

College and Marriage

The University of Illinois was a disappointment for Jesse. The white students would not allow black students to join their clubs or come to their dances. The football coach told Jesse that black students could not be **quarterbacks**.

Jesse heard about **demonstrations** in the South. Black people were beginning to **protest** the way they were treated. He decided to leave Chicago for North Carolina Agricultural and Technical College (NC A&T) in Greensboro, North Carolina. In those days, it was a mostly black school.

Jesse walks children to school in Chicago. He believes that all students should have a safe way to get to school.

This is a picture of Jesse and Jacqueline Jackson with their children.

Jesse was very popular at his new college. He was president of the student government. He joined a **civil rights** group called the **Congress of Racial Equality** (**CORE**). They organized demonstrations in Greensboro.

Jesse met Jacqueline Lavinia Brown. She and Jesse fell in love. They married while they were still students. They decided to spend their lives working for civil rights.

The Jackson Five

Jesse and Jacqueline have five children: •*Santita* •*Jesse, Jr.* •*Jonathan Luther* •*Yusef DuBois* •*Jacqueline II*

The Call

Jesse had never stopped going to church. But he had been too busy to think about his life after college. One night he dreamed that God asked him to become a **minister**.

Around that time, he met Dr. Martin Luther King Jr. He was a minister who taught people to hold peaceful **demonstrations** for **civil rights**. After he met Dr. King, Jesse wanted to be a minister more than ever.

During the 1950s and 1960s, Dr. Martin Luther King Jr. spoke out and led demonstrations for civil rights.

Dr. Martin Luther King Jr. and his followers marched for the right to vote in Alabama.

Jesse graduated from NC A&T when he was 22 years old. He decided to go to a school for ministers in Chicago, Illinois. Jesse and Jacqueline moved there with their baby daughter, Santita.

Jesse joined a civil rights group called the **Southern Christian Leadership Conference (SCLC)**. He began holding meetings about civil rights with teachers and students. When he was 24, he organized a group to join Dr. King in a march from Selma to Montgomery, Alabama. Dr. King noticed that Jesse was a good leader.

The Civil Rights Act of 1964

The Civil Rights Act of 1964 made it illegal to keep someone from voting, getting a job, or going certain places because of his or her sex, religion, or skin color. Many southern states refused to obey the law until the government forced them to do so.

Operation Breadbasket

Jesse left the school for ministers when he was 25 years old. He thought his work for the **SCLC** was important. Dr. King put Jesse in charge of Operation Breadbasket, a program to help black people get jobs and help black-owned businesses.

Jesse met with the owners of big companies and asked them to hire black workers for a decent wage. He also asked companies to buy things made by black-owned businesses. If the companies refused, Jesse organized **demonstrations** in front of their stores.

Jesse organized members of the SCLC to demonstrate in front of businesses that would not hire black workers.

Jesse speaks in his church in the old Capitol Theater in Chicago, Illinois.

Jesse was still holding his weekly **civil rights** meetings. Now hundreds of people wanted to join in. Jesse found an old theater that could hold a crowd.

When Jesse was 27, he became a **minister** and the old theater became his church. Soon, people could listen to his **sermons** on the radio. He often spoke in rhymes so that people would remember what he said. Jesse became famous.

15

The End of the Dream

Martin Luther King was killed at this motel in Memphis, Tennessee just a few minutes after this picture was taken. Jesse was 27 years old.

In early April of 1968, Jesse and another **minister** named Ralph Abernathy went to Memphis, Tennessee with Dr. King. They were planning to meet with workers there.

As he stood outside his motel room, Dr. King was shot and killed. Jesse saw everything from the parking lot.

When **riots** broke out after Dr. King's death, Jesse went on TV to remind people to behave peacefully. This upset some people in the **SCLC**. They thought Jesse was trying to take Dr. King's place.

Jesse went back to Chicago. He organized special fairs and celebrations. Some people worried that Jesse was becoming too powerful.

Ralph Abernathy asked Jesse to move to Georgia, where the SCLC had its office. But Jesse did not want to leave Chicago. Instead, he left the SCLC.

Some people thought Jesse would be the next Dr. Martin Luther King Jr.

PUSH

In 1971, Jesse announced that he was starting a new **civil rights** group. It was called People United to Save Humanity, or PUSH. In 1984, the National Rainbow **Coalition** was founded. Both PUSH and the Coalition would help poor people of all colors.

Two years later, Jesse heard about a **drought** in western Africa. PUSH helped raise money for the people there. Jesse traveled to Africa and began to learn about African history and culture.

Jesse told black people to be proud of their African roots. In this picture he is wearing African-style clothes.

Black people in South Africa were forced to live in houses that had no running water or electricity.

Jesse traveled to South Africa, which had laws to keep black people apart from whites. He met with American companies that did business in South Africa. He asked them to stop doing business there until the laws were changed. Jesse's work made many Americans realize that they had the power to help black South Africans.

Back home, Jesse realized that drugs were hurting poor people. In churches and schools around the country, Jesse told young students to keep away from drugs.

Run, Jesse, Run!

In 1983, Jesse heard that a United States **military** plane had been shot over Syria, a country in the Middle East. Jesse met with Syrian leaders and talked them into letting the pilot go free.

The next year, Jesse decided that it was time for the United States to have a black president. He tried to get well-known lawmakers to help him run for President of the United States. Only a few of them wanted to help him.

Jesse became very popular after he helped free pilot Robert Goodman in 1983. (Robert is the first man in the front row.) He thought that people would vote for him to become President of the United States.

Jesse led a march from Selma to Montgomery, Alabama twenty years after the one led by Dr. Martin Luther King Jr.

Jesse's **campaign** for president took him all over the United States. He did not win the election, but now he was more famous than ever. He spoke out for the **civil rights** of people all over the world.

He led a march from Selma to Montgomery, Alabama to show that some Americans still did not have equal rights. He met with the leader of the Soviet Union to talk about unfair treatment of Jewish people there. He led a march in Washington, D.C. to **demonstrate** for civil rights in South Africa.

Running Again

Jesse was still thinking about running for president. In 1988, he decided to try again. This time, many important lawmakers said they would help him.

Many other Americans said they would vote for Jesse, too. But at their convention, **democrats** chose Michael Dukakis for their **candidate**. Jesse hoped Dukakis would ask him to be his **running mate**.

People gather in support of Jesse at the Democratic Convention in 1988.

Jesse Jackson gives a speech supporting Michael Dukakis (right) and Lloyd Bentsen (left).

Jesse waited to hear from Michael Dukakis. Then, a reporter told him that Dukakis had given the job to someone else.

That night, Jesse made a powerful speech to the convention. Although he was hurt that he would not be Dukakis's running mate, Jesse promised to support him. He promised to keep working for **civil rights**. He said the United States was like a quilt made of many different fabrics and colors.

What's Next?

George Bush, Sr., beat Michael Dukakis. After the election, Jesse went back to Chicago. He began a **campaign** for black Americans to call themselves "African Americans." He thought this would be a way for people to honor their African roots.

Jesse spent a lot of time meeting with lawmakers in Washington, D.C. In 1989, he and Jacqueline decided to buy a house there. He was planning to run for mayor, but he soon changed his mind.

Jesse won many awards for his work. Many magazines carried stories about him.

Jesse had a TV Show called "Both Sides with Jesse Jackson." It was on the air from 1992 until 2000.

Two years later, the government of South Africa ended the laws that had been so unfair to black people. Jesse traveled there to meet with Nelson Mandela, a black South African leader. The white government had kept him in prison for more than twenty years!

Jesse also met with Saddam Hussein in the Middle Eastern country of Iraq. Several thousand people from other countries were in prison there. Jesse talked him into letting a group of 300 prisoners go.

Freedom and Fairness

Jesse helped watch over elections in South Africa when black people were finally allowed to vote there in 1994. In 1997, President Bill Clinton asked Jesse to **represent** the United States government in Africa.

Two years later, the United States was fighting a war in Kosovo, Yugoslavia. When some U.S. soldiers were taken prisoner, Jesse traveled there to help get them out of prison.

While he was in Africa, Jesse met with leaders of many countries. Here, he is meeting with Daniel Arap Moi, former president of Kenya, Africa.

Jesse marches in Washington to protest inequality in the workplace.

Jesse changed PUSH to the Rainbow/PUSH **Coalition.** He said that its new job was to make sure everyone was treated fairly in business. One place this was not happening was in the car business.

Rainbow/PUSH began working to make sure carmakers gave women better jobs. Jesse asked big car companies to help people of color open car dealerships.

Living the Dream

Today, Jesse Jackson still works with the Rainbow/PUSH **Coalition.** Wherever someone is not being treated fairly, Jesse is there, too. He makes people pay attention to things they would rather not think about. He reminds everyone that no one is free while some people live or work in bad conditions.

Jesse received the Presidential Medal of Freedom in 2000, the highest award for a United States civilian.

This is a picture of Jesse at a **demonstration** against war in 2003.

Rainbow/PUSH works to end diseases around the world. They have raised money to help people in countries where there have been storms or floods.

In 2004, Jesse gave a speech at Harvard University. He said that the Rainbow Coalition would keep working to make the United States a land of equal rights for everyone. Then, he said that all of us should work with other countries to make the whole world a better place.

Glossary

campaign   period of time during which a person works on a special project or runs for office

candidate   person who tries to get elected to a position in government

civil rights   things that all people should have, such as good jobs, homes, schools, and fair treatment

coalition   group of people that agrees to work together for one goal

Congress of Racial Equality (CORE)   civil rights group that began in Chicago in 1947

democrat   person who belongs to the Democratic National Party, a group of people who share similar beliefs about the way government should work. Every four years, they hold a big meeting called a convention.

demonstration   action in which people stand, sit, or march to show their feelings about something

drought   time of no rain when crops die

military   having to do with the army, navy, marines, or air force

minister   person who leads religious services

protest   to speak out against something that is unfair

quarterback   football player who tells the other team members what moves to make

represent   to speak for others

riot   disorganized fighting that breaks out suddenly

running mate   person who tries to get elected along with another candidate

scholarship money that is given to a person to pay for his or her education

sermon religious speech given in a church

Southern Christian Leadership Conference (SCLC) civil rights group that began in 1957 with the Montgomery, Alabama bus boycott and whose first president was Dr. Martin Luther King Jr.

Syria Middle Eastern country south of Turkey

More Books to Read

Jakoubek, Robert. *Jesse Jackson: Civil Rights Leader and Politician.* New York: Chelsea House, 2005.

Simon, Charnan. *Jesse Jackson: I Am Somebody!* New York: Scholastic, 1998.

Place to Visit

The National Civil Rights Museum

450 Mulberry Street

Memphis, TN 38103

(901) 521-9699

The former Lorraine Motel, where Dr. Martin Luther King Jr., was assassinated, has been turned into a museum of the history of the Civil Rights Movement.

Index